For Charlotta

PETER ZUMTHOR

1998–2001

Buildings and Projects

Volume 3

Edited by Thomas Durisch

Scheidegger & Spiess

Volume 1   1985–1989

What I Do

Volume 2   1990–1997

Volume 3   1998–2001

Poetic Landscape, Bad Salzuflen, Germany
1998–1999

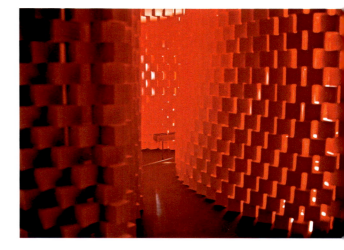

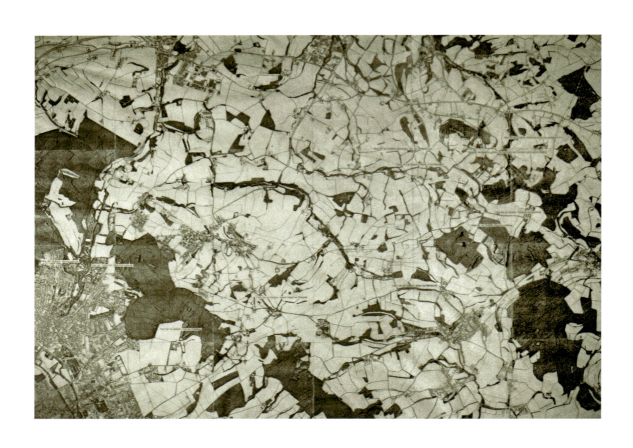

The Poetic Landscape project opened new spaces for me, new spaces to think about the connection of architecture to landscape and the creation of buildings that serve less a practical purpose than a spiritual need. I tried to design small houses dedicated to the reading of a poem, to the sound of a poem, to the presence of a poem written for a specific place in the landscape. The idea of a Poetic Landscape goes back to Brigitte Labs-Ehlert, director of the Literaturbüro in Detmold. She invited poets to write a poem for a specific place in the landscape and asked me as an architect to react to the places the poets chose with a house for the poem.

The region, the Lippe Uplands, an area east of Bad Salzuflen in North Rhine-Westphalia, barely twenty kilometers long and approximately twelve kilometers wide, plucked almost randomly from a larger landscape whole, was subjected to closer study and interpretation in the course of the literary and architectural work.

Anyone setting out to explore the Lippe Uplands, after the initial familiarization one needs to take in its understated forms of landscape, will soon discover places that are beautiful in their own way. The landscapes are quite literally remarkable, displaying their elements in succinct configurations and condensed images. At the same time, they do not feel so much unique or grand as they do characteristic and typical. What one finds here is a predominantly agricultural landscape, marked by generations of human labor. Here one sees growth through history, intensively worked land, landscapes overgrown or dying off, traces of neglect, decline, and change, as well as the new, both ugly and beautiful.

We searched the body of this landscape following the trail of places picked by the authors and found our own favorite places among them. We wanted to intensify the aura of these places through focused architectural intervention. In their totality, we hoped that these interventions would generate a wide-ranging energy field in the landscape. The various architectural and landscape constellations would coalesce into a new whole: houses meant for specific locations, houses meant in turn for particular poems, all having an impact on each other, a poetic landscape.

And so we devised buildings like large vessels, hollow architectural forms, created to capture the changing intensity of daylight and to foster new experiences from place to place: buildings made for lingering, reading, and speaking, created and built to trace the sound of the landscape.

The Poetic Landscape was never realized because the county government changed political parties. The stock of architectural images I dreamed of and worked on for this project later found expression in the Bruder Klaus Chapel in Wachendorf in the Eifel.

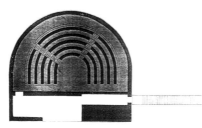

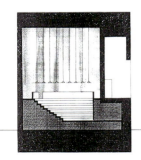

Zumthor House, Haldenstein, Graubünden
1998–2005

Living and working, family, children, grandchildren; spaces for living, spaces for working with younger colleagues, or inventing and planning buildings—to me these things belong together, and that is what the house was built for. It holds the main living spaces in three freely meandering linear sequences, interspersed with auxiliary spaces. When traversed in one direction, the spaces are increasingly work-oriented, or, in the other, they become more and more the private precinct of the family. The core of the architectonic composition is my south-facing studio, where I work with my back to a long wall, as I did in my first atelier. To the left, it leads up into the kitchen and to the right, into the living room, and if I face forward and walk around the inner courtyard, a grove of maples, I come to the rooms meant for working together with the architects and model builders who help me develop my buildings.

Some time before I built the house, we had done preliminary studies for different residences working with the idea of hollowed-out blocks. In the compositional principle of closed blocks and hollow spaces flowing freely into one another that characterizes the building today, there remains something of the sense of space that fascinated us back then.

The house is part of a little architecture colony that has gradually taken shape, since the late eighties of the last century, in this section of the Süsswinkelgasse. It is right next to the atelier built out of wood in 1986, the construction method of which is likewise an allusion to the wooden buildings of the village tradesmen. The new house is built of stone. The layer of textile we used to line the forms for the exposed concrete façades gives the house a soft, lively, and constantly changing gray color. The whole construction is meant to relate to the village structures that have emerged organically—the buildings, meadows, gardens, fences, and walkways—and it seeks intimate proximity to the steep slopes of ash trees that fall off to the Rhine valley below.

0   1   2   5

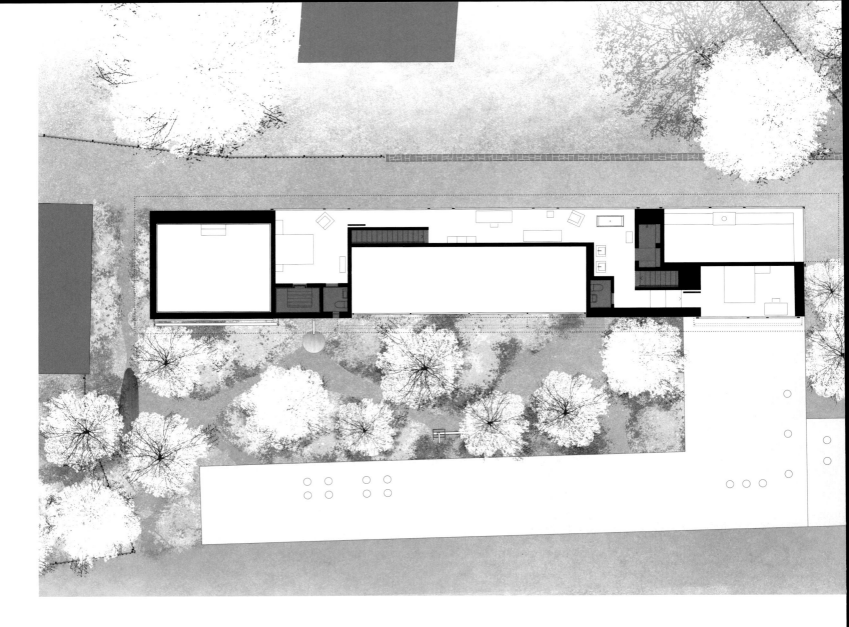

0 1 2 5

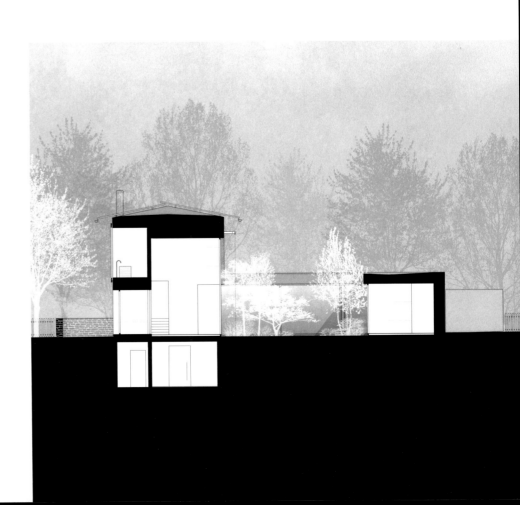

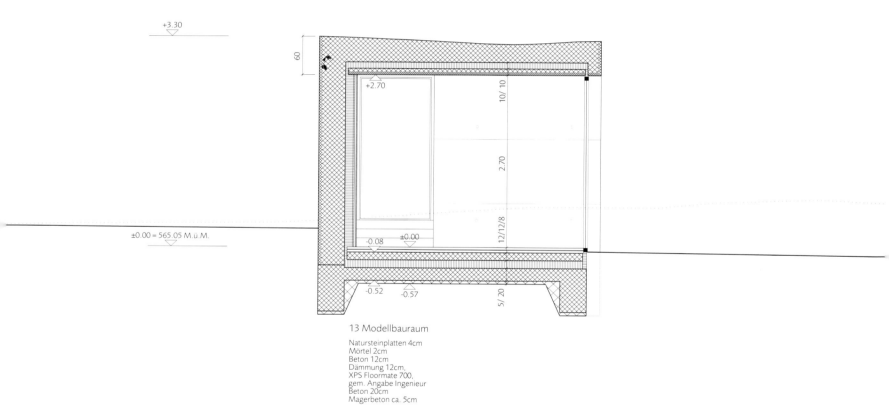

+3.30

±0.00 = 565.05 M.ü.M.

+2.70

10/ 10

2.70

12/12/8

−0.08   ±0.00

−0.52   −0.57

5/ 20

60

13 Modellbauraum

Natursteinplatten 4cm
Mörtel 2cm
Beton 12cm
Dämmung 12cm,
XPS Floormate 700,
gem. Angabe Ingenieur
Beton 20cm
Magerbeton ca. 5cm

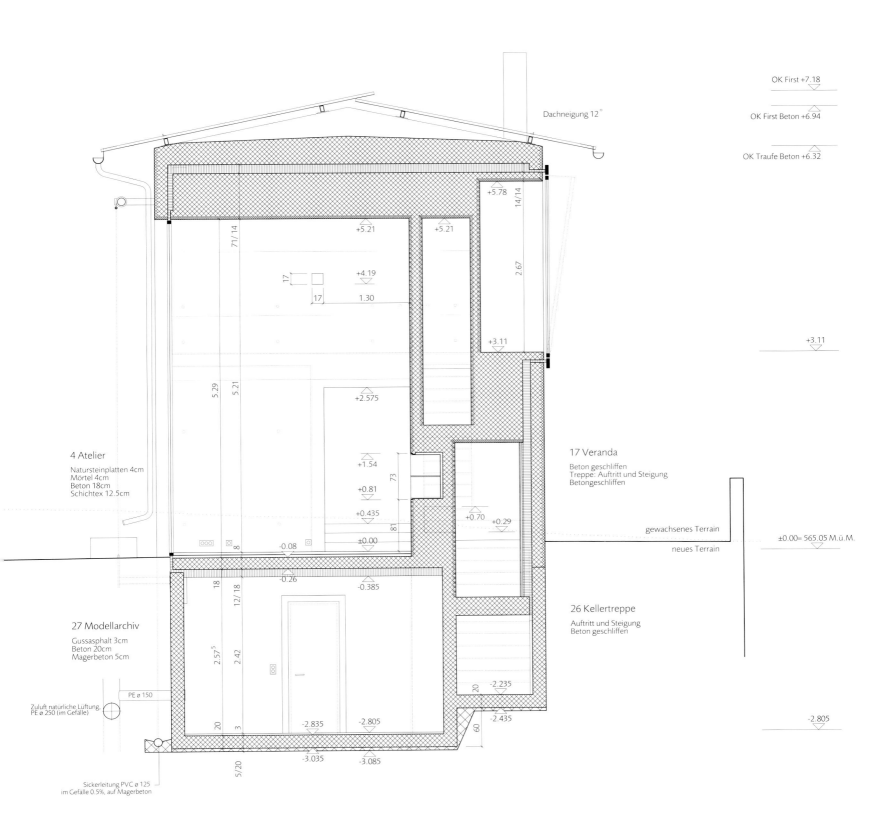

Dachneigung 12°

OK First +7.18

OK First Beton +6.94

OK Traufe Beton +6.32

+5.78

14/14

2.67

71/14

+5.21

+5.21

+4.19

17

17

1.30

+3.11

+3.11

5.29

5.21

+2.575

4 Atelier

Natursteinplatten 4cm
Mörtel 4cm
Beton 18cm
Schichtex 12.5cm

17 Veranda

Beton geschliffen
Treppe: Auftritt und Steigung
Betongeschliffen

+1.54

73

+0.81

+0.70

+0.29

81

+0.435

±0.00

gewachsenes Terrain

±0.00= 565.05 M.ü.M.

-0.08

8

-0.26

neues Terrain

18

-0.385

12/18

26 Kellertreppe

Auftritt und Steigung
Beton geschliffen

27 Modellarchiv

Gussasphalt 3cm
Beton 20cm
Magerbeton 5cm

2.57⁵

2.42

-2.235

20

Zuluft natürliche Lüftung,
PE ø 250 (im Gefälle)

PE ø 150

-2.435

-2.805

60

20

3

-2.835

-2.805

-2.435

5/20

-3.035

-3.085

Sickerleitung PVC ø 125
im Gefälle 0.5%, auf Magerbeton

Mountain Hotel, Tschlin, Graubünden
1999–2002

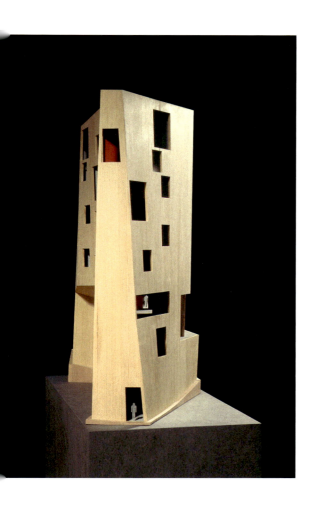

The Engadine is a region loved by many. It is a high Alpine valley with extra-ordinarily beautiful old villages and a bright blue sky. According to local legend, the Engadine's sgraffiti-decorated Baroque farmhouses with their funnel-shaped windows inspired Le Corbusier in his creation of the chapel at Ronchamp. There was a strong hotel tradition in the Engadine around 1900, from Sils-Maria through St. Moritz and down to Tarasp-Vulpera. Since that time not much more has happened in the building culture of the Engadine.

So for that reason we were surprised and excited when the small community of Tschlin asked us to come up with a plan for a hotel in the village and to suggest a suitable building site. We attempted to conceive the hotel from inside out, so to speak, with a view to its unique assets: the region's natural products and people from the valley to operate the hotel. It was a small cultural gesture, a way for the hotel to stay "itself" while attracting the world. The watchwords that would guide us in the project were: simple, natural, cultivated—small but elegant.

We envisaged a hotel and an architecture that would incorporate the under-lying harmonious beauty of the landscape with houses that had developed over centuries and was miraculously still intact. We dreamed of a new intensity: cosmopolitan, contemporary, unprecedented, unheard-of. We wanted to create a new destination, but one that would be inconceivable without the history, the landscape, the people of the region and their culture.

Our architecture project for Tschlin was basically a cultural one. The shape of the building we devised for this job, its cellular structure and sculptural response to the landscape generated mental images in me that have stayed with me and inspire me still. One of these images is of the distinctive "plumage" made of hand-split larch that sheathes the sculpted shape of the building rather like wooden shingles.

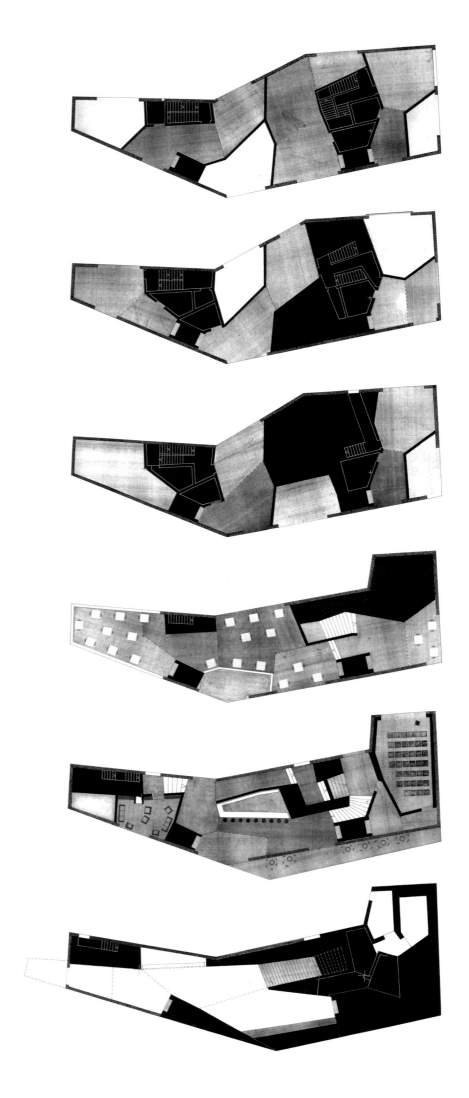

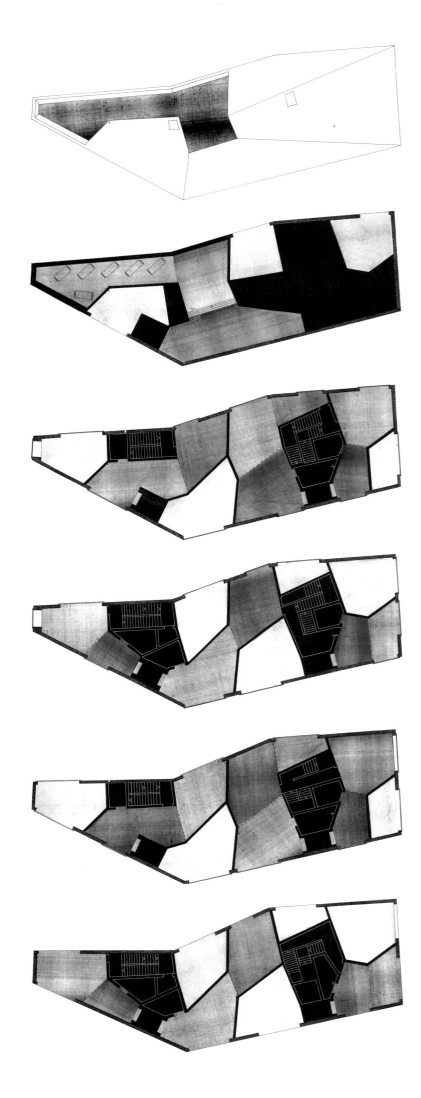

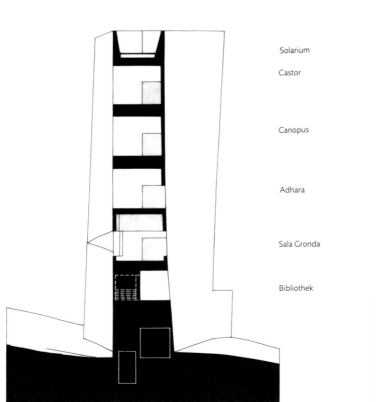

Solarium

Castor

Canopus

Adhara

Sala Gronda

Bibliothek

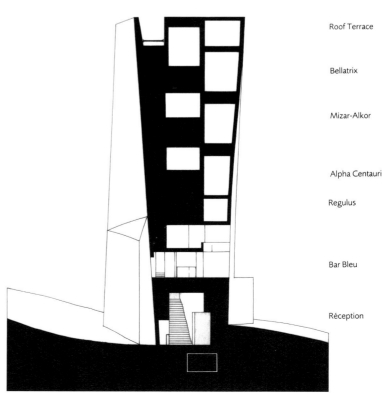

Roof Terrace

Bellatrix

Mizar-Alkor

Alpha Centauri

Regulus

Bar Bleu

Réception

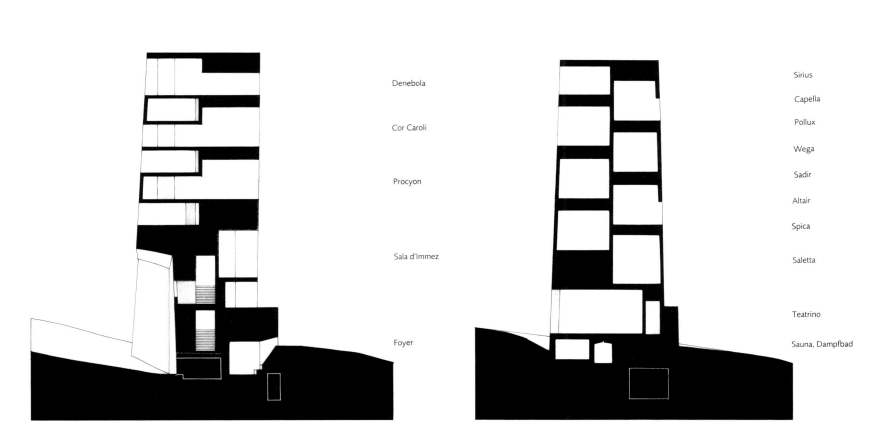

Denebola

Cor Caroli

Procyon

Sala d'Immez

Foyer

Sirius

Capella

Pollux

Wega

Sadir

Altair

Spica

Saletta

Teatrino

Sauna, Dampfbad

I Ching Gallery, Dia Center for the Arts, Beacon, New York, USA
since 2000

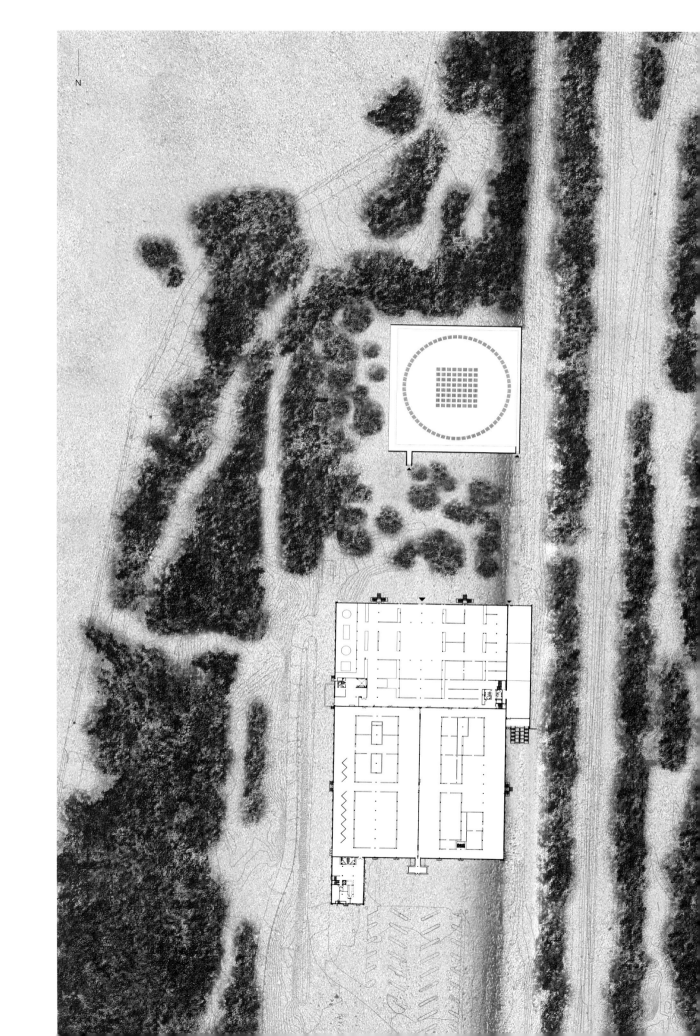

We designed the I Ching Gallery as a permanent exhibition space for Walter De Maria's sculpture of 1981, which he called *360° I Ching / 64 Sculptures*. The planned location was an open area behind the Dia:Beacon museum in Upstate New York.

The sculpture is based on the hexagrams of the I Ching, a classical Chinese text, known as *I Ching—Book of Changes*. The hexagrams, each consisting of hexagonal rods laid out in square fields of six continuous or broken lines, are on the floor and take two forms: one a large white square and one a large black circle surrounding the white square. The sculpture requires an unbroken space of about 70 square meters, with good natural light conditions. Contemplation of the work should not be disturbed either by supports or by direct sunlight. The building is like a large container formed out of monolithic concrete. The roof is bonded to the walls and consists of a supporting grill about five meters high, which reflects the daylight. The direct light of the sun is diffused by the supporting beams of the roof. Atmospheric changes in the natural lighting from sunrise to sunset, in summer and winter, are reproduced inside the building on the bright mineral surfaces of the roof supports and the walls that reflect and disperse the light. The whole effect is authentic and direct; the building has a natural presence.

Visitors enter the structure via a gallery, a hollow space cut into the western and southern outer walls that leads gradually down to the level of the sculpture. The circuit around the sculpture is accomplished through two low walkways on the eastern and northern sides of the main level: these, too, are recesses in the mass of the surrounding walls. In this way it is possible to view the sculpture from different angles, from above and from the side, before finally walking into the sculpture spread out on the floor, into the space between the 128 black-and-white quadrants. The magic of the experience is materialized geometry, seen up close. The building, conceived as a closed shell for a single sculpture in open natural light, has a large window on the eastern side. This opening toward the east was important to Walter De Maria, as was the relationship of the interior to the landscape. Walter was a critical accompaniment to my design and when he was in Haldenstein, he told me that he would campaign to get a permanent home for the I Ching sculpture. The work was important to him, he said, and he wanted people to see it. Walter De Maria died on July 25, 2013, a year after his visit. His work has taught me that abstract geometry can have a sensual presence.

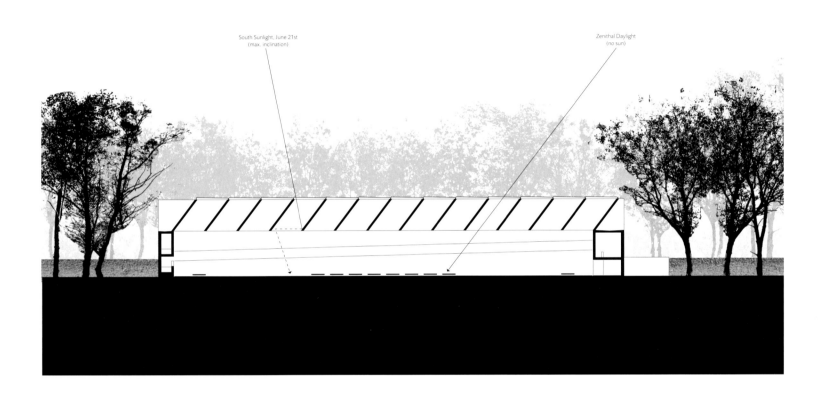

South Sunlight, June 21st
(max. inclination)

Zenithal Daylight
(no sun)

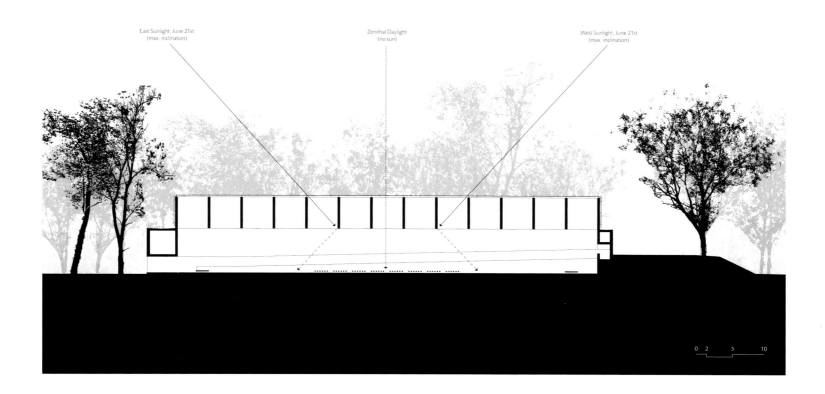

East Sunlight, June 21st
(max. inclination)

Zenithal Daylight
(no sun)

West Sunlight, June 21st
(max. inclination)

0 2 5 10

Harjunkulma Apartment Building, Jyväskylä, Finland
2001–2004

: 100

In the Finnish city of Jyväskylä a large piece of land became available next to the covered market hall. A beautiful building was to be erected there for some 160 comfortable city apartments, along with social facilities and businesses on the ground floor. The city administrators wanted to set a standard for good architecture. They wanted to show that the town could not only host an international Alvar Aalto symposium every three years, where architects from all over the world discuss their work, but that they could still seize the opportunity to develop new architecture. Alvar Aalto went to school in Jyväskylä, where he built beautiful houses, a workers' club, a theater, and university buildings.

Unfortunately, the city government that commissioned us to do the study had already contracted the land to a major, semi-public residential construction firm before we had started working on our design. Only later did we discover what that meant for the project. The firm's managers initially let us proceed with the design, but in the end they insisted on their own conventional ideas: they wanted the project to be divided up into two or three separate buildings; they insisted on having them built in two consecutive stages, and they wanted to see at least six apartments per staircase and floor. Beyond that they also insisted on compact, so-called cost-effective construction, meaning buildings of substantial depth and bulk with apartment floor plans extending deep into the building's interior so that, more often than not, only the narrow sides of the rooms faced the building's façade.

The heart of our design was a large common courtyard. We saw the birch tree branches drifted with snow and the water of the pond in the courtyard turn to ice in the Finnish winter; we saw children skating and heard the first birds singing in spring. We envisioned this courtyard as a secluded interior space for the whole residential community.

The apartments we sketched were bright and sleek. They are laid out along the façade, so the rooms have a veranda-like feel. The public rooms are open-plan and the space is continuous from façade to façade, from the courtyard to the city. The nine entryways to the apartments are on the protected inner courtyard and are "attractive addresses," with every entryway built a little differently and not too many doorbells per entry. The building style is airy and light.

Our project did not find favor with the people running the construction firm. To save it, we reworked the floor plans and the city architect had a market analysis done proving the project's cost-effectiveness and sustainability. An experienced Finnish real-estate saleswoman praised the layout of the apartments, and renowned Finnish architects offered their support. Alas, all in vain: the construction company's executives didn't want to go down any new roads.

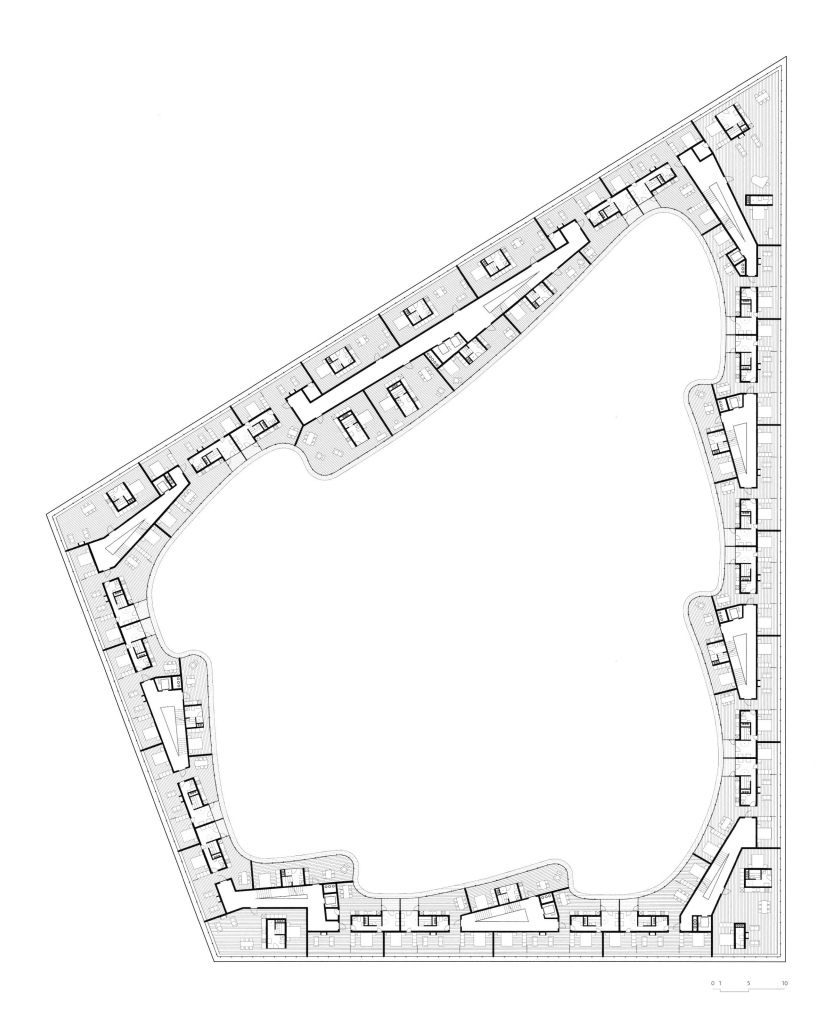

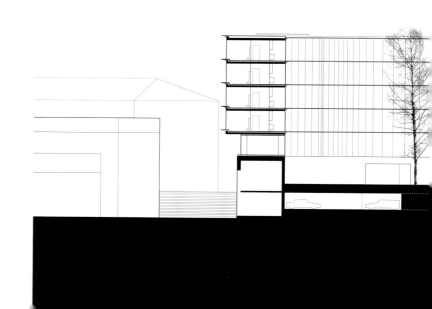

Pingus Winery, Valbuena de Duero, Spain
2001–2005

The winery was designed for a small, high-end producer in the Duero Valley in Spain. The winery was not to be a plain, rectangular factory with an imposing façade, but a workplace in the countryside. We viewed the building as an instrument of production: one should know by looking at it what it produces and why it is there—this was the design concept.

Vehicles, machines, equipment, storage tanks, barrels, bottles, everything needed for wine production, are gathered together under one roof. The tractors with their trailers filled with freshly harvested grapes drive up and the work starts.

The fruit was to be brought into the new building and the wine produced in the most natural way possible. The grapes were to be delivered to the upper level so that the pressed juice would later flow down into the tanks below without mechanical pumps and then further down into the barrels and the bottling area. The storage area for the barrels was to be on the ground floor, with no air conditioning. The slope of the site was to be used to let the flow of the grapes and the wine benefit as much as possible from gravity.

The landscape of the Duero Valley near the village of Monasterio is inspiringly expansive and has a hot breath that cooks the grapes. The dream of building for this landscape a winery that would provide shade and shelter, as large and natural as a farm, remained unfulfilled.

terrain + roof

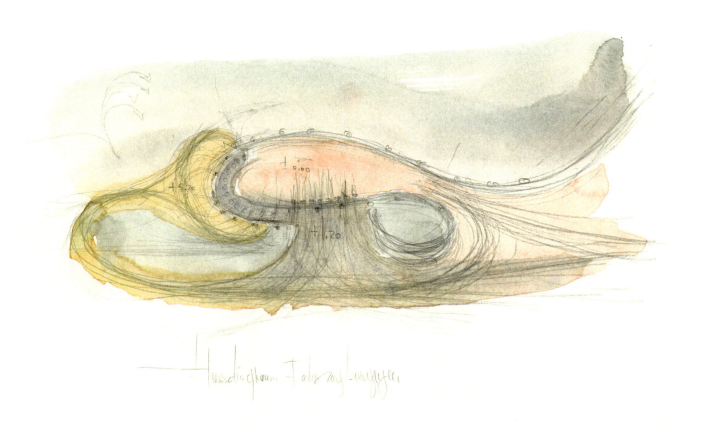

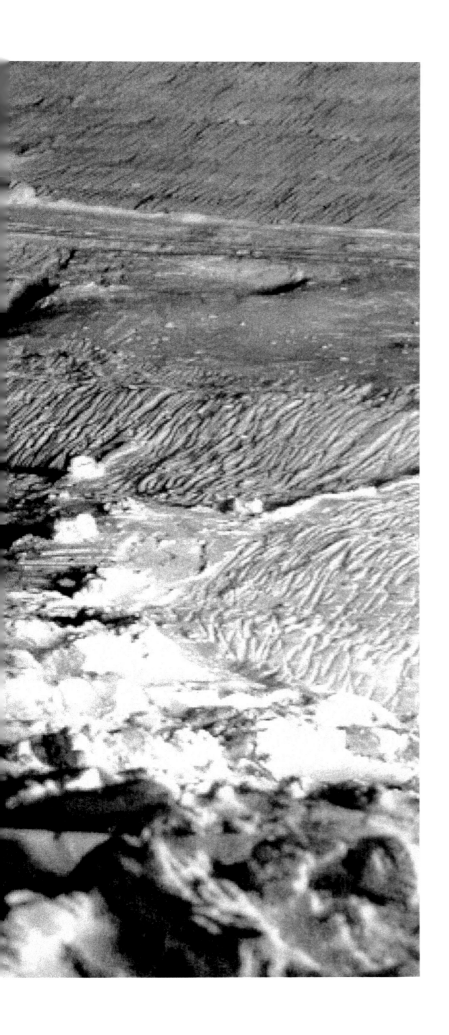

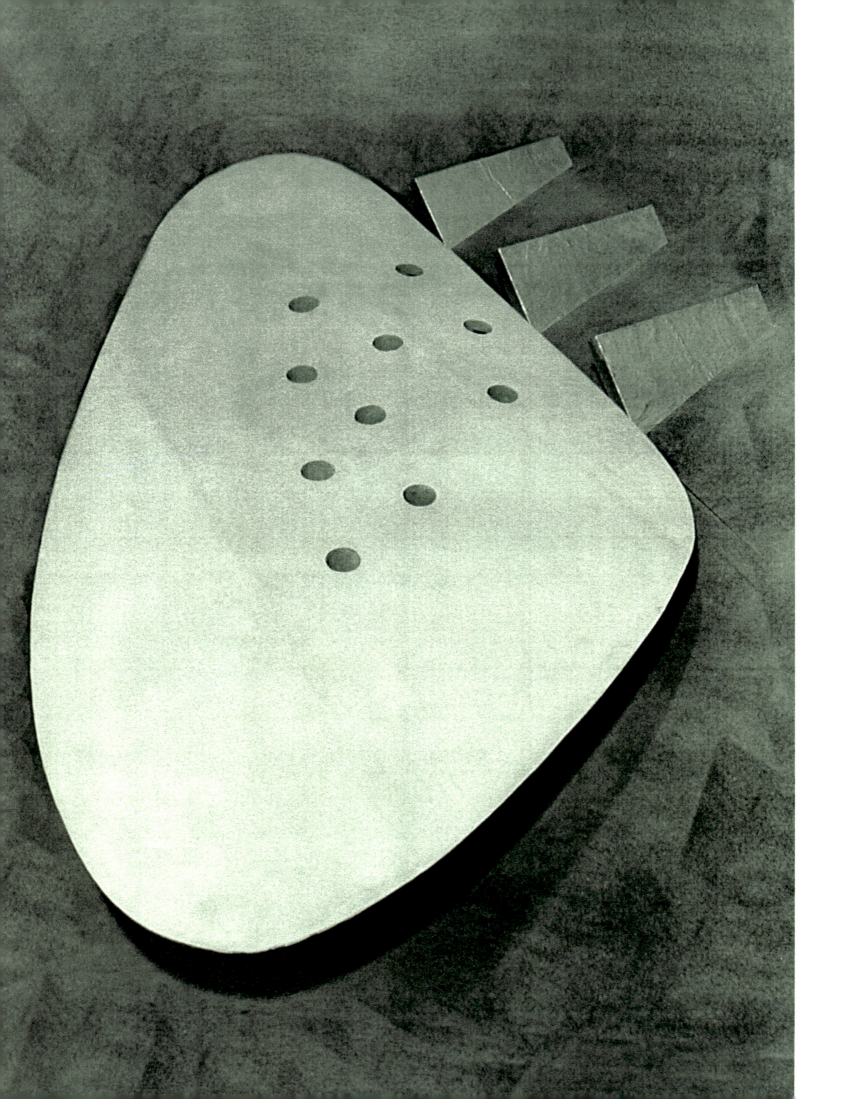

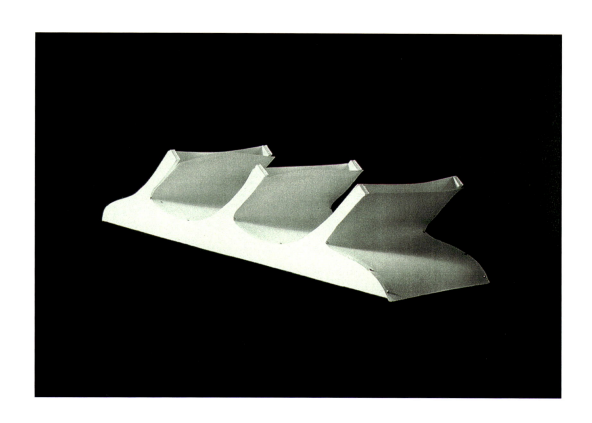

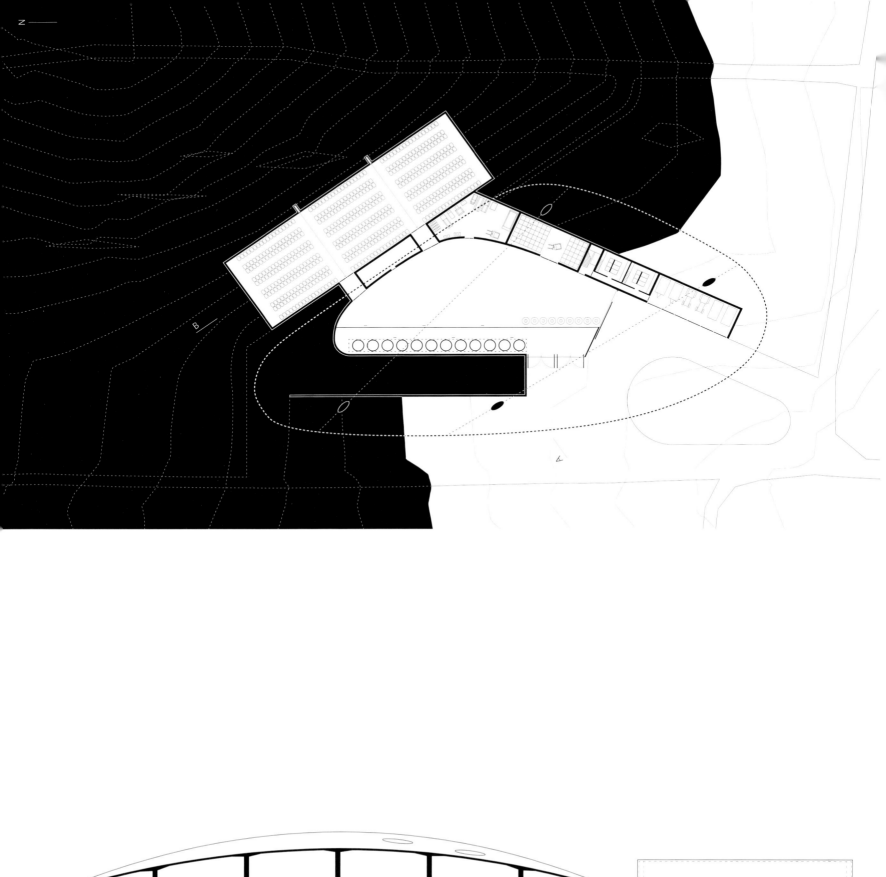
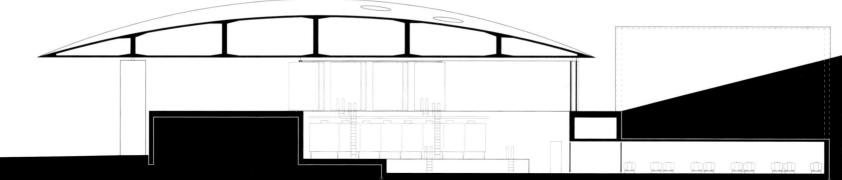

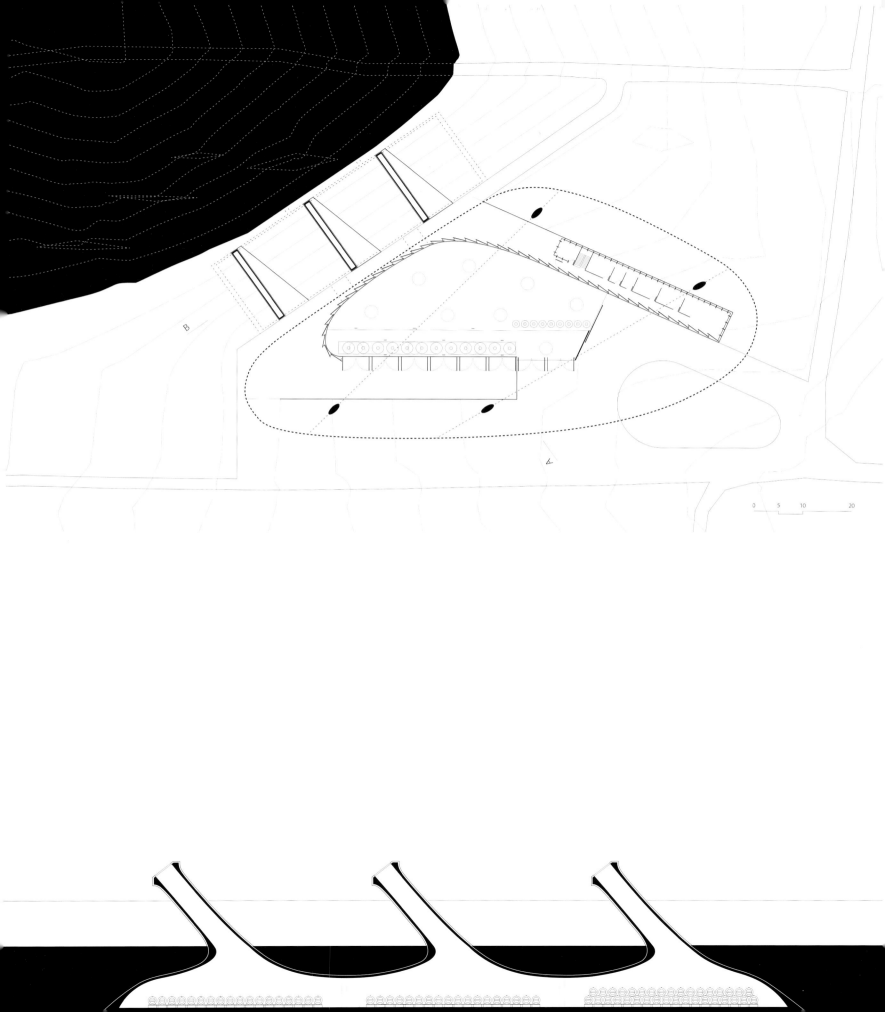

B

0   5   10   20

Bruder Klaus Field Chapel, Wachendorf, Germany
2001–2007

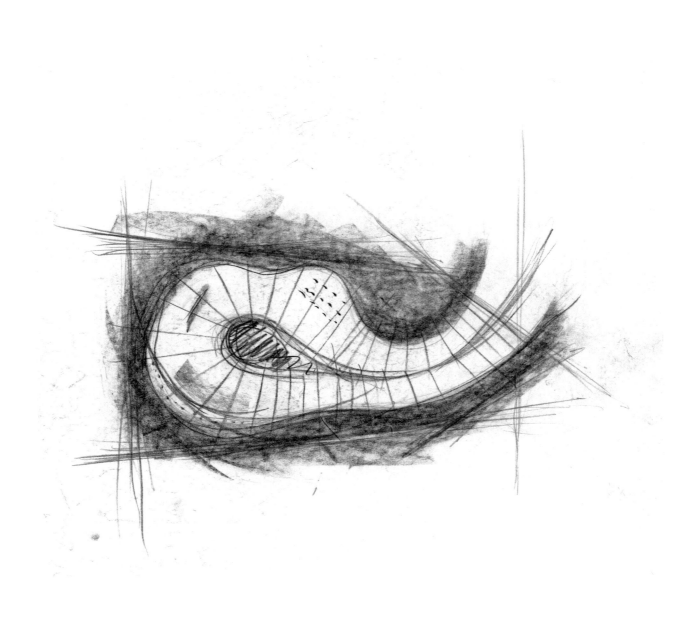

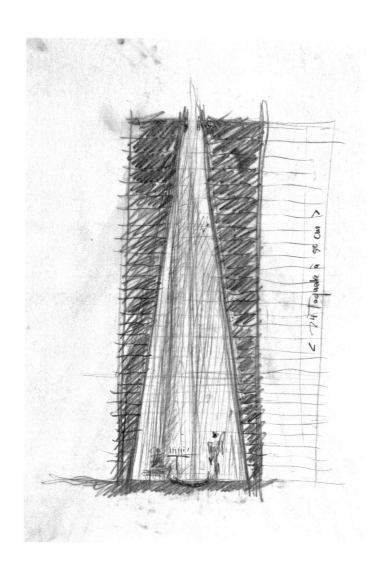

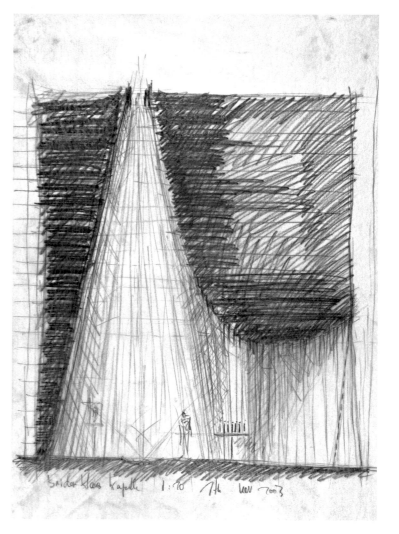

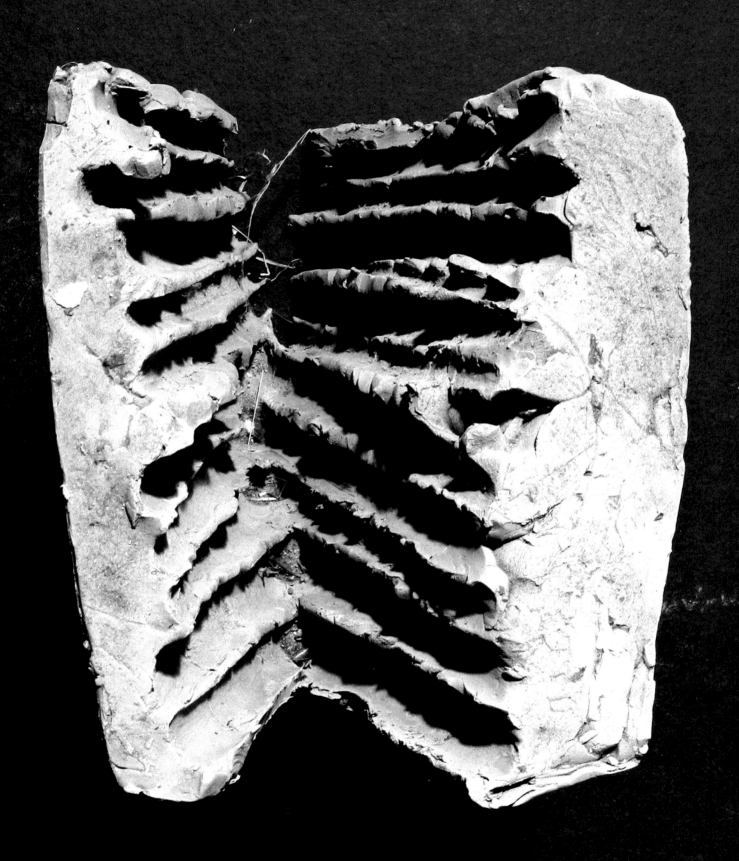

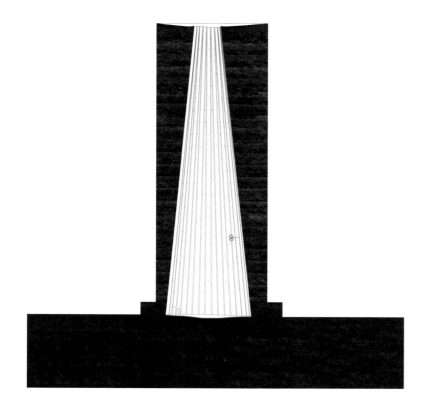

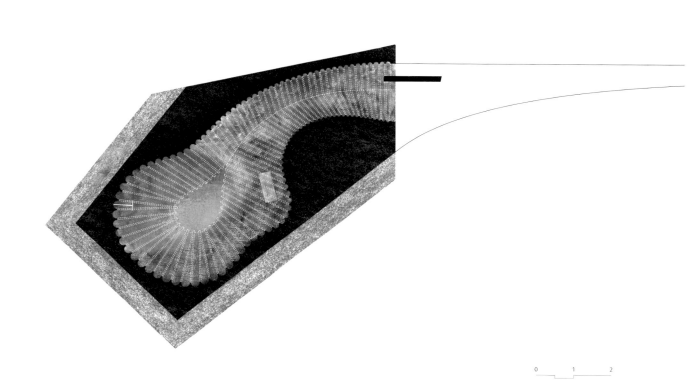

A tower appears in the countryside above the little village of Wachendorf in the Eifel. It changes our perception of the landscape; it creates a new point of reference; landscape and tower start to connect. I am thinking of the bridge in an essay by Martin Heidegger that suddenly comes into view as the first structure in a pristine river valley; it defines the place, giving it a left and a right, an upper and a lower, something it never had before.

The germ cell of the design for the Bruder Klaus Chapel can be found in the "poetry houses" (individual structures designed to relate to a specific poem) I had worked on two years before in the context of the Poetic Landscape project. I was actually unaware of this connection while working on the chapel. It was only later, after the chapel was built, that Brigitte Labs-Ehlert, the author of the Poetic Landscape Project, pointed out the similarity of the spatial innovations in both projects.

It took years for me to find the right interior for the little field chapel. In time, the design became clear and elemental: light and shade, water and fire, material and transcendence, the earth below and the open sky above. And then, suddenly, the little devotional space became mysterious. A stroke of luck.

The mystic, Bruder Klaus, whose real name was Niklaus von Flüe, lived in central Switzerland from 1417 to 1487. He was not canonized until the late twentieth century, but he is a sort of household saint to me: he was important to my mother, who says that he often helped her in difficult situations. I myself was impressed by the straightforward, uncompromising character revealed in his biography. It was perhaps this personal background that led me to agree to the request of the two Eifel farmers Hermann-Josef and Trude Scheidtweiler to build a chapel dedicated to Bruder Klaus on their field above the village.

I had a free hand in the creation of the chapel. My design concept and the prolonged process of trial and error before finding the right form were somewhat demanding on the Scheidtweilers. They let me decide things, but wanted to do as much of the building as possible themselves, to keep the costs low. So they themselves cut and trimmed 112 tree trunks as instructed and then, with the help of friends and the guidance of a carpenter, up-ended them to form a huge wooden tent. On each of twenty-four work days, they packed a fifty-centimeter-high layer of rammed concrete all around the wooden tent. When finished, the twenty-four layers of concrete had reached a height of twelve meters. Then, the client set a slow fire that burned for three weeks inside the wooden tent, which was now the inner formwork of the concrete surround. The tree trunks shrank in the smoldering fire, which blackened the walls with soot. When the fire finally went out, the scorched tree trunks were removed, leaving behind their imprint and the lingering smell of smoke.

The interior space hidden inside the five-sided tower was given a very simple liturgical treatment in keeping with the client's wish: a small bronze wheel with three spokes pointing inward and three outward, which is the symbol that Bruder Klaus is said to have used in meditation, and a bronze cast of a head mounted on a stele by Hans Josephsohn that Hermann-Josef Scheidtweiler believes resembles the saint. The chapel is a place for personal meditation, not a consecrated place of worship for religious services. To me, that was the right thing to do, as I wanted the chapel to have an open form that would hint at existential questions.

Additional Cabins, Pension Briol, Barbian-Dreikirchen, Italy
since 2001

The Pension Briol in Italy's South Tyrol, an 1898 mountain inn renovated
by the painter Hubert Lanzinger in 1928, is a secret tip for those who
want an uncomplicated summer vacation in the mountains. This inn, at an
elevation of 1,300 meters above sea level, is an hour's hike from the
village of Barbian. In its way, Briol is a total work of art in miniature. My
1994 essay "From a Passion for Things to the Things Themselves" has
a chapter devoted to the marvelous variety of spatial situations inside and
outside this mountain inn.

Pension Briol is a mountain inn in the old style. The two guest rooms can
be heated with wood stoves. In the bedrooms, washbasins and water
jugs stand on wooden tables, like in days gone by. Simple baths and toilets
are found in the hall. All this has style and charm, and the owners of
the house want it to stay that way.

But there are also guests, for instance, families with children, who want
heated guestrooms with en suite baths. It was our task to create these units.
Any expansion of the main house was out of the question, as it is under
historic preservation; neither could it be affected by any new construction in
its immediate surroundings. So gradually the idea took shape of having
free-standing single buildings somewhat away from the main house:
five light wooden cabins connected by footpaths, set freely into the slope
and partially enveloped by trees at the forest edge. Little boardwalks
lead from the paths to these "tree houses" hovering in the treetops on stilts.
The cabins are covered by flat, single-pitch roofs of board shingles. The
topography of the slope remains unchanged; the natural vegetation, incursions
of mountain pastureland penetrating the forest edge, and bushes and trees
are preserved.

The five buildings vary to suit the needs of different guests. The solitary seeker
of tranquility, the couple with a baby or several children, two couples who
are friends staying together, or the large family with grown children—all of
them will find the right accommodation for their stay. Various living,
working, and sleeping options are available. There is a small wood stove in
the living area and a small cooking facility as well. The little cabins are
winterized.

Common to all of them is a high-ceilinged living room fronting a large
terrace with a view of the Dolomite mountains across the valley, which gleam
in the evening sun and over which the sun rises in the morning.

146

Forat 5. Nov. 05

4 x 2.60 = 10.4 m²
4 x 2.60 = 10.4 m²
4 x 3.0 = 12. m²
Total 33 m²

Schnitt 1:100

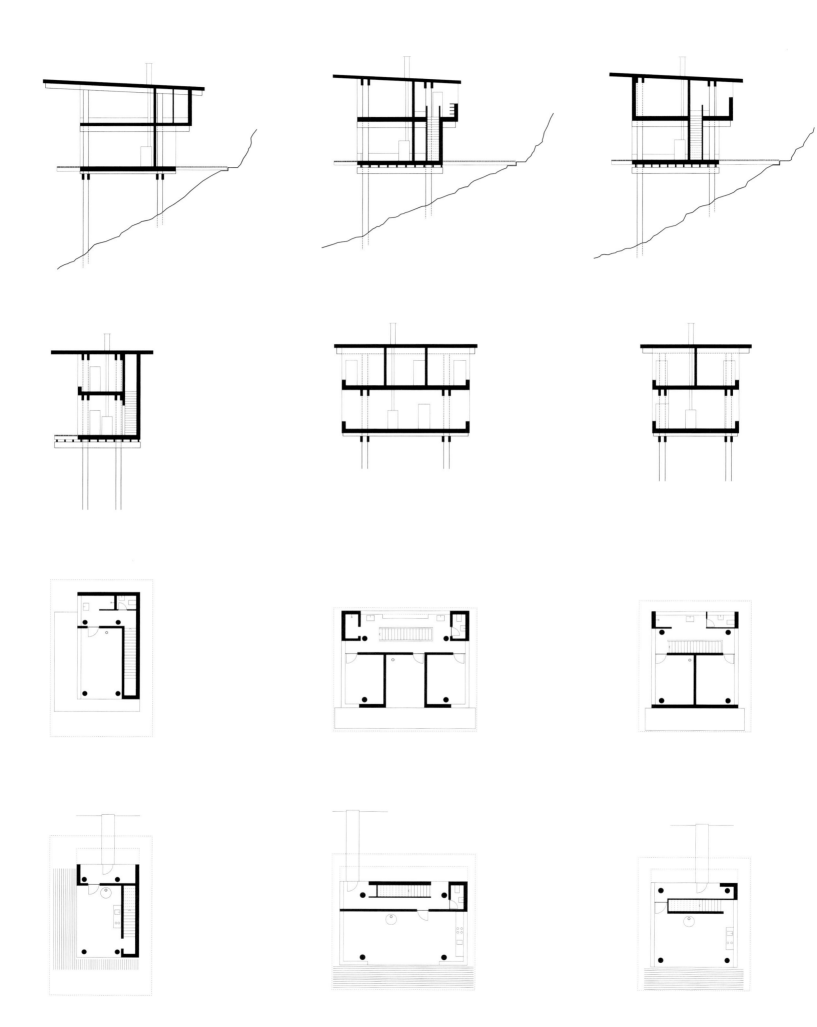

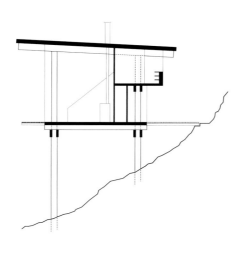

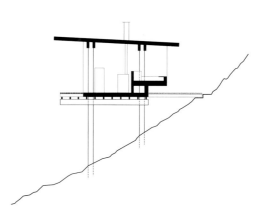

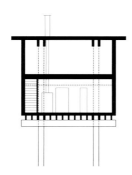

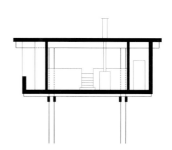

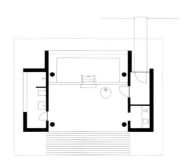

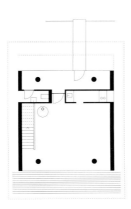

0   1   5   10

Concept: Peter Zumthor, Thomas Durisch, Beat Keusch
Design: Beat Keusch Visuelle Kommunikation, Basel – Beat Keusch,
Angelina Köpplin
Artistic advice: Arpaïs Du Bois
Translation: John Hargraves
Editing: Catherine Schelbert
Proofreading: Bronwen Saunders
Image processing: Georg Sidler, Samuel Trutmann
Printing and binding: DZA Druckerei zu Altenburg GmbH, Thüringen

Picture credits, see appendix, volume 5

This book is volume 3 of *Peter Zumthor 1985–2013,* a set of five
volumes which are not available separately.

© 2014 Verlag Scheidegger & Spiess AG, Zurich

New edition 2024: ISBN 978-3-03942-248-7

German edition: ISBN 978-3-03942-247-0

Verlag Scheidegger & Spiess AG
Niederdorfstrasse 54
8001 Zurich
Switzerland

Scheidegger & Spiess is being supported by the Federal Office of
Culture with a general subsidy for the years 2021–2024.

www.scheidegger-spiess.ch